The HOPIS

Pueblo People of the Southwest

BY VICTORIA SHERROW

NATIVE AMERICANS
THE MILLBROOK PRESS
BROOKFIELD, CONNECTICUT

Cover photo courtesy of National Museum of the American Indian (no. 2284)

Photos courtesy of National Museum of the American Indian: pp.
6, 21 (no. 4181), 29 (no. 3485); Photo Researchers: pp. 11 (©
J.H. Robinson), 50 (© Jim Carter); New York Public Library Picture
Collection: pp. 15, 31; Bettmann Archive: pp. 17, 36, 46; Museum
of Northern Arizona: pp. 22 (neg. no. 10217), 32 (neg. no. 93C.1,
Owen Lowe), 51 (left: neg. no. 79.2371, Mark Middleton; right:
neg. no. 84C.2, Horizons West); University of Southern California:
pp. 25, 41; Milwaukee Public Museum: p. 45.

Map by Joe Le Monnier

Library of Congress Cataloging-in-Publication Data

Sherrow, Victoria.
The Hopis : Pueblo people of the Southwest / Victoria Sherrow.
p.   cm.—(Native Americans)
Includes bibliographical references and index.
Summary: Presents the history and culture of the Hopis, from their
earliest years on the North American continent to the present day.
ISBN 1–56294–314–6 (lib. bdg.)
1. Hopi Indians—Juvenile literature. [1. Hopi Indians.
2. Indians of North America.] I. Title. II. Series.
E99.H7S52   1993
978′.004974—dc20   92–45055   CIP   AC

Published by The Millbrook Press
2 Old New Milford Road, Brookfield, Connecticut 06804

CONTENTS

Facts About the Traditional
Hopi Way of Life 5

Chapter One
"Little People of Peace" 7

Chapter Two
Life in a Traditional Hopi Village 13

Chapter Three
Arrival of the "Lost White Brother" 35

Chapter Four
Hopis Today 47

A Hopi Creation Story 55

Important Dates 57
Glossary 59
Bibliography 60
Index 62

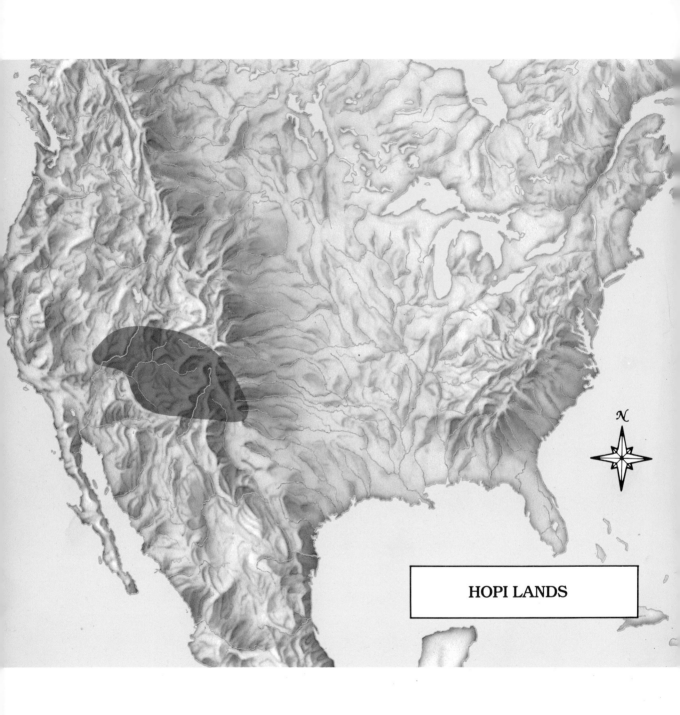

HOPI LANDS

FACTS ABOUT
THE TRADITIONAL HOPI
WAY OF LIFE

GROUP NAME:
Hopitu

DIVISIONS:
Hopi and Tewa-Hopi

GEOGRAPHIC REGION:
Southwest—Arizona, Colorado, New Mexico

LANGUAGE:
Aztec Tanoan

HOUSE TYPE:
Rectangular adobe houses, or pueblos

MAIN FOODS:
Corn, squash, beans, wild plants

*The mesa village of Walpi was founded at the
end of the seventeenth century. Hopis used ladders
to move from one house to the other.*

Chapter One

"LITTLE PEOPLE OF PEACE"

It was an unusually dry summer in the American Southwest. Each day, the Hopis stared uneasily at the cracked, powdery earth in their small cornfields. Hourly, they prayed that rain would fall to soften the ground. Even in less dry seasons, the Hopi people worried about rain. The average fall of rain and snow was only about 12 inches (30 centimeters) per year. There were no lakes or rich, natural supplies of water on Hopi lands—only an occasional spring or a small, often dry riverbed.

Water meant food and life, as every Hopi knew from a young age. Describing his childhood in the book *Sun Chief*, Don Talayesva wrote, "I also learned that water is as precious as food. Everyone appeared happy after a rain." Without enough rain, the corn would not grow; people would die.

Asking the Cloud People and other gods for the blessing of rain has been part of Hopi ceremonies, prayers, and dances for centuries. An important Hopi chant includes these words:

Ho wondrous water
Ho wondrous water
Giving new life to the drinker . . .
Giving life to the people.

Besides pleasing the gods through prayer, the Hopis believed in working hard and living in balance with nature. They tried to follow the peaceful "Hopi way." The word Hopi came from the name they gave themselves: Hopitu, meaning "peaceful ones."

The Hopis lived at the westernmost edge of a large culture group called the Pueblo Indians. For thousands of years, their ancestors were scattered throughout the American Southwest. The Hopis eventually settled in what is now Arizona.

Hopi villages were built on flat-topped hills, or *mesas* ("table" in Spanish). Surrounding these mesa villages lay Hopi land, which spread across the high, rugged Colorado Plateau in the Middle Rio Grande area. The Painted Desert was found there, as was the spectacular Grand Canyon, the deepest canyon on earth. With its turquoise skies and desert hues, Hopi country—called the Land of Enchantment—was unique in all the world. For centuries, the Hopis felt attached to their land and way of life despite the shortage of water.

Long ago, the Southwest was less dry. Archaeologists—scientists who dig up ancient dwelling places to learn how people lived—think the first Native Americans came from Asia to North America some 30,000 years ago. Small groups of people probably crossed the Bering Strait between Russia and Alaska. Perhaps a land bridge across the strait let people walk across, or they may have come in small boats. Large animals, such as the bison and woolly mammoth, were already roaming the continent. Early hunters used simple stone and bone weapons to kill these towering beasts for food and clothing.

The ancient peoples who moved south found swamps and forests where elk, bison, antelope, bighorn sheep, and other game animals roamed. These distant ancestors of the Pueblo Indians moved about in a large area that included present-day Nevada, New Mexico, Arizona, Utah, and Colorado.

Gradually the climate of America changed. Glaciers (thick sheets of ice) began to melt. The weather grew warmer and drier. The woolly mammoth became extinct (died out) between 6000 and 4000 B.C.

To survive, people learned to eat new foods. They gathered seeds and wild plants: acorns, pinyon nuts, grass seeds, mesquite beans, and yucca fruit. They ate the flesh of cactus plants and used the shells to store liquid. In the southwestern deserts lived rats, mice, rabbits, snakes, lizards, and insects they could catch and eat.

The life-style of the people during this period from 6000 B.C. to about A.D. 1 is called the Desert Culture. Desert Indians moved around to find food and water, living in caves or outdoors. They wove sandals and baskets from the desert grasses. Baskets were used for gathering seeds, nuts, roots, and berries and to store food in the winter.

From this Desert Culture came several groups of Indians who developed different ways of life throughout the Southwest. One group, called the Anasazi (from a Navajo word meaning "ancient ones"), were the Hopis' direct ancestors. The early Anasazi were called Basket Makers. Archaeologists think that during the first century A.D., the Anasazi stopped moving about. They settled in caves in the Four Corners area, where the present-day states of Arizona, Utah, Colorado, and New Mexico meet.

By digging up thousands of Anasazi caves, archaeologists have discovered bodies of men about 5 feet 4 inches (163 centimeters) tall and shorter women. The men had long hair, while women's hair was often cut short. Since hair has been found in Anasazi mats and nets, it seems likely that women cut their hair to use for weaving material. The Anasazi learned to raise corn (maize), which grew well in a hot, dry climate such as theirs. They also grew squash and beans.

Skeletons of crippled and old people have shown that the Anasazi cared for the elderly and sick. The Anasazi believed in life after death, for the graves held spears, pottery, baskets, ears of corn, clothing, and other things for use in the afterlife. They also smoked cane cigarettes, probably during religious rituals.

From about A.D. 400 to 500, the Anasazi left their caves and built large stone multi-family houses called *pueblos*. The people who lived in them came to be known as Pueblos, too. Most pueblos had from five to twenty rooms, but some had hundreds. Villages had square or oval pit houses for religious rites. For the next few centuries, people built up their communities. They improved their crops and tools, wove clothing from cotton, and made shell and turquoise ornaments.

For some reason, maybe a bad drought, these people left their villages during the 1200s. The Kayenta group of Pueblos moved south into Arizona and became the Hopis. They were a small group, numbering only a few thousand when the Spaniards came in the 1500s.

Pueblos were often tucked into the sheer sides of cliffs for protection. The circular pit house can be seen in this Anasazi ruin on Colorado's Mesa Verde.

From 1300 to 1540, the Hopis built new mesa towns and developed a special way of life. New generations heard ancient tales in the Hopi language, which comes from the Aztec Tanoan group of Native American languages. Hopi children heard how the "ancient ones" first came to earth from an underworld. According to Hopi belief, three times the ancients had been given a world to care for. But they had been selfish and had not respected the plants or animals, so they lost all three worlds. Massau, the keeper of the fourth world, told them to prove they deserved a new place to live.

The ancients wandered for years before they settled in the desert, amid four mountains. From a hill, they got instructions from the Star People. Hopi legend says these people first lived in Kawestima, in a smaller canyon of the Grand Canyon. Today this place, named Betatakin Ruin, is preserved by the National Park Service.

The farming life of the Hopi was hard in a dry land. Yet by working together, they prospered. A stable food supply led them to create an orderly way of life. As the sun rose and fell each day and the seasons changed, nature gave rhythm to Hopi life. Harmony with nature and with each other helped the Hopis survive in a difficult land and through times of great hardship. This desire to live in peace has remained at the heart of Hopi culture to the present day.

Chapter Two

LIFE IN A TRADITIONAL HOPI VILLAGE

As an early morning sunrise glowed above the desert plateau, a Hopi village crier called people to their daily chores. Men began walking down the long trails that led to the edge of the mesa. At the end, near the scarce sources of water, were small fields of corn, beans, squash, and melon. Women began preparing food, caring for children, making pottery, and doing other household work. Older children helped their parents, knowing there would be time for play later on. For everyone, prayers, part of their spiritual way of life, began early in the day.

The Hopi belief in a harmonious and spiritual connection to nature showed in the design of their villages. Their walled cities surrounded a central plaza, or village square. In the plaza were pit houses called *kivas*, where men gathered for ceremonies, for instruction in Hopi ways, and to learn how to do crafts.

There was no central tribal leadership. Each Hopi village governed itself, led by a village chief (*kikmongwi*) and his advisers. The role of chief was inherited. Villages were divided into halves, each with its own kiva. One half was for the Summer People; the other for Winter People. These halves were, in turn, divided into smaller groups, or clans. Clans often had the names of animals, such as Bear, Lizard, Antelope, or Badger. Clan membership came from the mother, and each village clan had its own smaller kiva. Hopis could change their given names but not the clan into which they were born. As children, Hopis learned to identify with their clan.

HOMES ▪ Hopi homes, or pueblos, were four- to five-story rectangular apartment buildings with flat roofs. Walls were shared, and the floor of one room was the roof of the room below. Men built homes out of flat slabs of sandstone—a rather soft rock with a red or yellow color common in northern Arizona—and adobe, a kind of mud. These tight, compact units could shelter an entire town.

People lived in the outer rooms, where more sunlight came through. On the balconies and terraces, people cooked and made pottery, wove, or ground corn. Inner rooms were used to store food or to live in during the colder seasons.

Furnishings were simple. A stone- or clay-lined fire pit was dug into the middle of the room. The smoke rose up through a hole in the roof. Small alcoves in the walls held religious statues and other objects. Women built small shrines to the household gods. A wooden pole or length of yucca fiber was strung from the ceiling to hold clothing. People could sit on built-in stone benches. They slept on blankets on the floor. Rolled up by day, these blankets became extra seats. There were also simple farm tools, such as digging sticks and hoes, and stone tools the

The walls of this Hopi home are made of
adobe, and the brush, grass, and mud ceiling
is supported by heavy wood beams. Dried corn
is stored at left, and at right is a work area.

women used to grind corn. A food storage bin stood nearby. Various baskets and clay pots were ready to be used for cooking and storing food.

WOMEN AND MEN ▪ Women owned the houses and household goods. They also owned food, seeds, and any water that was stored or located in the springs. The Hopis respected marriage and family life. Most people were married and had only one partner. Women were allowed to tell their husbands to leave, but most marriages lasted. A woman could will her home to a child or grandchild, male or female. In that way, men could become home-owners.

Men usually lived with their wives and children. They did not punish their children, although they gave them advice. Sometimes a woman's brother lived with her, and it was he who disciplined her children. A married woman might also live in her mother's home with her children. Men kept their religious clothing and objects at their mothers' homes.

Women and men had separate chores, but both harvested food. Men hunted animals and prepared the skins for clothing and moccasins, which they made. Hopi men made bows, arrows, and shields, and they spun cotton thread and wove fine blankets and sashes. They also did heavy work, such as carrying firewood and the stones needed to build homes.

A man's main job was to provide food, mostly through field work. The Hopis did not think people could *own* land. But village councils divided the land so that each man had enough to feed his family. Individual plots came from the land assigned to the clan and village group the men belonged to. A man who failed to use his land might lose it to his clan or to his nephews.

FOOD ▪ Springs were scarce, so fields were small, sometimes only 4 or 5 square feet (.4 or .5 square meters), and located wherever there was water. Hopi men planted seeds deep in order to take advantage of any moisture in the ground. Some men walked miles a day to tend their fields, weeding and pulling off worms and insects that might hurt their crops.

"Hopi Woman," by William R. Leigh.

FRIED PINYON NUT CAKES

Ingredients:

2 cups pinyon (pine) nuts
$^3/_4$ cup water
$^1/_2$ teaspoon salt (optional)
Vegetable oil for frying

Chop the nuts. Then roll them under a rolling pin until they turn into coarse meal. Mix the crushed nuts with the water and salt, making a firm dough. Set the dough aside at room temperature for an hour. *Heat oil in a heavy skillet. With a tablespoon, drop the dough onto the hot skillet. Cook on low heat until brown on each side. (Makes about 6 cakes)

FRIED CORN CAKES

Ingredients:

$^3/_4$ cup corn (fresh kernels or thawed, frozen corn)
$^1/_4$ cup flour
$^1/_2$ teaspoon baking powder
Salt and a dash of black pepper, to taste
1 large egg, well beaten
Oil for frying

*Heat the oil in a heavy skillet until it is hot enough, about 350 degrees. Mix the corn, egg, flour, salt, and pepper. With a teaspoon, drop the batter into the hot oil and cook until golden brown all around. Drain on paper towels and eat. (Makes about 24 cakes)

*Have an adult help you fry these cakes.

Corn was the main food. Besides the yellow or white ears commonly found today, the Hopis grew blue, red, purple, black, and speckled corn of different sizes. At harvesttime, wives often gave food to their husbands' families. Some food went to the village council to aid widows, orphans, the needy, and village guests. Many Hopi women hung four ears of corn—yellow, blue, white, and red—in the house. These colors stood for the four directions—North, South, East, West—from which the Hopis believed their clans had come when they settled on the mesas.

Besides corn, the Hopis raised several kinds of beans and squashes, melons, and tobacco. Sunflowers were also grown for the oil in their seeds.

At planting time, ceremonies were held in the fields. The men planted the first seeds, using digging sticks like those of their Anasazi ancestors. Nearby, the women sang in low voices. The Hopis believed that women must take part in the planting, or crops would not grow.

Women sometimes raised beans in fields near their homes. Some also tended fruit trees or vines outside the village. Women owned these crops, and they had to cook and preserve the food that came from them. Fresh food was available only at harvesttime. The rest of the year, people ate dried, stored foods. It took days to grind corn and nuts by pounding them with a hand stone called a *mano* on a larger, flat stone called a *metate*.

With their limited foods, the Hopis made interesting and healthful dishes. Like the Aztecs and other Central American peoples, they made cornmeal pancakes and filled them with meat or beans. Soups were made from squash blossoms, beans, or meat, or sometimes with corn dumplings.

The Hopis made several different kinds of bread. *Piki* was a thin bread made from ground blue cornmeal. Women mixed water and a pinch of sage ashes with the cornmeal to make a paste. They spread it on a greased rock that had been heated over a fire. The batter baked quickly into a wafer like bread that was folded and left to dry. Another special bread was *chukuviki*. Small loaves of this ceremonial bread were made by steaming dough in corn-husk wrappers.

Animal meat added variety to their mostly vegetable diet. Hopis hunted gophers, squirrels, antelope, deer, and mountain sheep. Animal sinews (the tough tissue that joins bones and muscles) made good bowstrings; the bones became various tools. Even the hooves were saved to make rattles for ceremonies.

Rabbits were common in the region. Men and boys went on group hunts. To trap rabbits, they stood in a loose circle around a wide area. They would move closer together, keeping the animals inside an ever tighter and smaller circle. Then they shot them with arrows or struck them with sticks. Besides the meat, rabbits offered hides that made soft, warm robes.

CLOTHING ▪ Rabbit-skin robes had clothed Pueblos for centuries. To make them, skilled weavers first cut the skins into thin strips. Then they wove the strips with plant fibers to make a strong cloth. These warm rabbit blankets were highly prized for winter wear.

People without fur capes wore feather blankets over the simple cotton clothing that Pueblos had made since ancient times. Pueblos were the only Indians north of Mexico to use cotton cloth. Hopi shirts were simple pieces of cotton with neck holes. Sandals were made of woven plant fibers.

In this watercolor by Narron Lomayaktewa,
men place willow sticks, antlers, an animal skull,
and broken pottery at a hunt shrine for good luck.

Summers were hot. Men usually wore a simple cotton loincloth, with a cloth sash tied around the waist. Women wore a rectangular piece of cotton cloth that covered the right shoulder, then fastened under the left arm, leaving the left shoulder bare. They tied woven belts or sashes around their waists several times to hold the dress in place. Hopi children under the age of ten usually wore no clothing during hot weather.

MARRIAGE ▪ Hopis had strict rules for courting and picking marriage partners. Girls chose the boys they would marry during group rabbit hunts. They took corn cakes to the hunt and traded them for rabbits. By giving her leftover cakes to one boy, a girl showed that she had chosen him for courting.

This Hopi bride is leaving her mother-in-law's house with her
second wedding robe in her arms. She will wear this at her death.

The boy then discussed the matter with his parents. A few days after the hunt, the girl sat outside her house, perhaps grinding corn, waiting for the boy to visit. If he came, the courting began. During courting, the girl still played the leading role. If she took a basket of *piki* bread to the boy's home, it meant that she wanted to marry him. To agree to the marriage, the boy ate the *piki*, sharing it with his male relatives.

Weddings were festive. The men in the groom's family, usually his uncles, had the job of weaving the bride's white wedding robe with red, black, and green trim. They wove another white robe for the bride to carry to the ceremony. This second robe would cover the bride when she died and went to the Spirit World.

Another tradition involved corn and baskets. The Hopi bride and her mother made many baskets and filled them with cornmeal. The bride visited her future mother-in-law, bringing baskets of corn as a gift. The groom got the largest basket. When he died, this basket was buried with him.

One custom was both fun and messy. The families of the bride and groom had a mud fight in the village square before the wedding. During this ritual fight, the relatives were allowed to make jokes about each other. This pretend fight was viewed as a good way to help the families get rid of any bad feelings before the marriage. This custom has continued in modern times.

Before the ceremony, the bride and groom had their hair washed at the same time by each other's relatives. A special shampoo for this purpose was made of soap from the roots of the datil yucca plant. For centuries, the Hopi had known how to pound the yucca roots to get a soapy liquid. The bride and groom often stood side by side, their soapy hair mixed together, to show they would soon be joined as one.

A grand feast marked the wedding day. Sacred cornmeal was used to make a line called the "trail of life" from the groom's home to the bride's. At dawn, the couple walked to the eastern part of the mesa. They breathed upon some sacred cornmeal and said a prayer as they threw cornmeal toward the rising sun. When they returned to the village, they were married. In some villages, a Hopi priest told the newlyweds how important their union was to themselves and to the village. He told them "not to be foolish or argue" and to "live in harmony."

CHILDREN ▪ Most married couples looked forward to having children. A woman who was expecting a child obeyed rules the Hopis thought would lead to an easy birth and a healthy child. She wore loose clothing and kept her hair untied. She did not hold children on her lap or walk behind people on the street. She avoided looking at snakes so that her baby would not twist itself into the wrong position or come out feetfirst.

The father was careful to treat all living things kindly so that no harm would come to his child. A man also brought weasel meat home for his wife and rubbed her with weasel fur. These customs were thought to help the baby come out of the mother quickly, as a weasel springs from its underground hole.

At birth, babies were washed in warm water and rubbed with juniper ashes. The Hopis thought this kept a child from growing too hairy. Some sacred cornmeal was touched to the infant's mouth. The grandmother marked the four walls of the room with cornmeal for good luck.

For nineteen days, mother and child stayed indoors. During this time, a fire burned day and night to keep away bad spirits.

Before dawn on the twentieth day, the naming ceremony began. The father's female relatives gathered at the home of the mother's grandmother to decide on the child's name. The baby was bathed and rubbed with cornmeal. Each woman blessed the child by dipping a well-shaped ear of corn, called Mother Corn, into cornmeal and water. The child was then given his or her name.

Hopi babies were treated with much gentleness and affection.

Relatives came to see the baby, who was taken outside for the first time. The baby's father announced the first signs of the rising sun. The godmother and mother carried the baby to the edge of the mesa. They prayed as they raised the baby up to glimpse the sun. The newborn was introduced to the Sun Father by calling out the child's name. People feasted on *piki* bread and other special foods.

Hopi babies usually spent most of the first six months of their lives on padded wooden cradleboards. Wrapped in a cotton blanket and strapped to the board, they were safe and could be carried about and placed on tables or against walls while the mothers worked. Cradleboards were used by the Hopis and other Indians for centuries. Wooden ones have been found in Anasazi caves. The board pressed against the back of growing heads, giving them a flatter shape than they would otherwise have had. The shredded and pounded juniper or cedar bark that padded the boards was also used for diapers.

When they were about six months old, babies were allowed to move about. They learned to crawl and, later, to walk. As they got older, Hopi children played and explored freely in the village. They had dolls and toy animals made of clay or cornhusks. They ran foot races and kicked balls or sticks. In a game called *we-la*, several players used feathered darts, each choosing a different color. Carrying these darts, they chased a child who held a small hoop made of corn husks. The object of the game was to throw the darts through the hoop. The person who tossed the most darts through the hoop won.

Children roamed the pueblos safely, with many adults to watch out for them. Parents expected their children to learn about nature, not to injure animals or people, to be kind, and to respect the elderly. At an early age, Hopi children began to watch the grownups, learning how to do the chores that would be theirs one day.

In his book *Sun Chief*, Don Talayeswa wrote that Hopi children thought that copying adults was "like play." He wrote, "We followed our fathers to the fields and helped plant and weed. The old men took us for walks and taught us the use of plants." Girls joined their mothers to gather seeds, grasses, and nuts or to dig up clay for pottery. Everyone had to do their share. Talayeswa said, "The old people said that it was a disgrace to be idle. . . ."

Children were rarely hit, yelled at, or punished for behaving badly. They knew the rules and did not want to embarrass themselves and their families. If mild scoldings did not work, a parent might warn a child that an evil spirit would come to take him or her away from the pueblo.

Children learned early about different spirits and the Hopi outlook on nature and daily life. Children took part in group religious ceremonies. As teenagers, Hopi boys joined kivas and learned about their secret ceremonies. Kivas were underground, circular rooms, usually made of stones. A ladder or steps led down to the entrance. Sacred religious objects, including clay figures, drums, and rattles for chanting, were kept under guard in the kivas. Young children were forbidden to go in. When they were old enough to join a kiva society, boys were warned not to tell any secrets they learned there.

During the winter months when crops were not being tended, boys who were old enough sat in the warm kivas to hear stories told by Hopi elders. These men passed on the Hopis' ancient history and beliefs. Here the boys learned how to prepare and dress for ceremonies and learned the words of the chants and prayers. They were shown how to do men's work—spinning and weaving cloth, preparing leather hides, and making tools.

RELIGION ▪ In past centuries, Hopi men may have spent about half of their time taking part in religious activities. The Hopi religion included a view of both the light and dark—good and evil—sides of human existence. The Hopis had long believed in good helper spirits, as well as bad witches and demons. Many of the religious rites taught in the kivas were about calling on the good spirits to bring rain to their dry land. In the summer, people prayed for rain and a good harvest. Winter prayers were devoted to health, fertility, and peace.

Kiva groups had the duty of performing Hopi dances on special occasions. One or more priests (holy men) led the preparations for sacred dances. Each kiva guided some aspect of religious life. One might perform ceremonies to help farming, while another did healing dances, and still others led rites to aid hunting or bring rain. The men used special prayer sticks, costumes, and other objects. These ceremonies are still held today and often have a strong effect on those who watch them.

The important masked kachina dances were held from December to July. *Kachinas* (also written as katsinas or katzinas) were believed to be supernatural beings or gods who lived in the San Francisco Peaks near Flagstaff, Arizona, and in springs, lakes, and bodies of water. Ancient legends said that the kachinas came to earth, singing and dancing to bring the Hopis joy. To help the Hopis, the kachinas brought gifts and taught them farming, hunting, and arts and crafts.

Masked kachina dancers and a clown in stripes weave through a village. The dancers visit children to find out if they have been good, and they punish them if they have not.

After leaving the earth, the helpful kachinas still blessed deserving humans with health, rain, good crops, and peace. Other kachinas were naughty or monstrous spirits who scolded misbehaving humans. It was thought that at death every Hopi became a kachina. So, the kachinas symbolized the spirits of Hopi ancestors, a link between the people on earth and the beings in the Spirit World.

The Snake Dance

The Hopi Snake Dance is one of the most famous of all Native American ceremonial dances. It is held for nine days in late August, beginning when the moon is full. The mesas are usually dry then, and people fear that fire or lack of water will kill their crops. In the Snake Dance, the Hopis honor their ancestors and their beginnings, and they pray to the God of the Clouds.

Members of the Snake and Antelope societies perform the dance. It lasts only about thirty minutes but takes more than a week to prepare. Priests spend the first eight days of the ceremony holding secret prayers in their kivas. On four of these days, the Snake priests search the desert for snakes, hoping to capture some from each of the four directions—North, South, East, and West. The priests prefer rattlesnakes, but they will take other types, including red racers and bull snakes, if rattlesnakes cannot be found.

On the afternoon of the ninth day, the Snake and Antelope priests get ready for the dance. They wear face paint and special ceremonial skirts and ornaments and carry rattles. The colors of the paint and clothing have symbolic meaning. Yellow stands for pumpkins, green for corn, and red for fruit.

The drum beats a steady rhythm as the priests and dancers enter the square. At the village plaza, the Antelope priests shake gourd rattles as they sing and dance. The Snake priests dance in groups of three, one holding a snake in his mouth while another strokes it with a special wand.

Snake dancers encircle a ring of sacred
cornmeal at Mishongnovi, 1901.

The traditional wooden wands have pictures of snakes on their green handles and eagle feathers at their tips. They seem to quiet the snakes during the ceremony, perhaps because eagles are enemies of the snake.

People who have seen this dance, still performed today, wonder why the Hopi dancers seldom get bitten. The priests do not remove the snakes' fangs or give them drugs. Perhaps they avoid harm by their confident handling of the snakes and by their skillful use of the eagle-feather wands. Equally impressive is a rainfall soon after a Snake Dance ceremony.

Men and a few women dressed as kachinas, wearing fancy sacred masks and costumes during the ceremonies. There were about two hundred of them, often named for animals, such as Eagle, Badger, Hummingbird, Owl, Wolf, Snake, and Bear. Other Hopi groups believed in kachinas with names such as Long-Haired Kachina, Spotted Corn, Black Ogre, and Mudhead. Kachinas had an important place in the Hopi religious beliefs that were part of day-to-day life.

CRAFTS ▪ About two hundred years ago, wooden dolls were first made in the likeness of kachinas. Kachina dolls were not sacred but were tools to teach children about religion and to help them learn their ancestors' names. They were carved from the roots of dead cottonwood trees, then given masks painted to look like certain kachinas. Some were remarkable works of art, with carefully cut eyes, noses, ears, and horns. Kachinas might wear colorful costumes and feathers and carry swords, rattles, bows and arrows, and other objects.

Hopinyu Kachina of the Hopi Coyote Clan.

Kachina doll-making was fairly new among the Hopis, but they had been skilled basket makers for thousands of years. Grasses were woven into trays, bowls, gathering baskets, water-tight cooking and storage baskets, and sifting baskets. Weaving styles differed from village to village.

Skilled basket makers used many patterns and colors. Coiled baskets were the most tightly woven and were used during traditional Hopi weddings. The base of a coiled basket was a spiraling piece of stiff grass or plant stem. Softer grasses of many colors were added as the basket was woven. For twined baskets, two strands of material were woven into a base of other strands. A third method—plaiting—used flexible reeds and grasses.

Hopi pottery has been admired for centuries. Ancient pottery was made of gray clay. Some pieces had a woven pattern, made by pressing a basket against the wet clay. Later pieces had black-on-white designs. A black dye was made by boiling sunflower seeds and adding gum from the pinyon pine tree. Squash seeds, saffron flowers, sumac berries, alder bark, and metallic ores also provided colors for paints. Rich reds, golds, oranges, and yellows were popular. White clay was used as white paint. The leaves of the yucca plant and rabbits' feet were used as paintbrushes.

The potter began by rolling the clay between her hands into long ropelike coils. Then she wound the coils to form bowls, jars, or other objects of different heights and shapes. A flat piece of wood was used to smooth the clay piece inside and out. Traditional potters still use this method.

Clay containers allowed Hopis to store food and water for a long time. Corn and seeds stayed fresh in clay jars. Pottery and basketry let women show their talent in creating geometric designs, lines, swirls, and figures. Birds were popular, perhaps because they were thought to fly between the earth and the Spirit World above. Hopi murals and early pottery show legendary birds and animals that resemble those of the Tlaloc religions practiced in Central America. This suggests some early contact between these peoples.

DEATH ▪ Old people were respected and were as active and useful as their health allowed. They played an important part in raising children.

When death came, people were sad but did not mourn for a long time. The dead person's body was washed and dressed in clean clothing, and spirit feathers were put in one hand. A woman wore the second white robe she had received at her wedding. A man's digging stick and wedding basket were put in his grave. Death was part of the cycle of life. A person's spirit went to an underground world called *Sipapu*. There, he or she joined the Spirit World as a kachina.

After a funeral, people did not speak the dead person's name, so he or she could move freely into the Spirit World. The living then went back to their duties within their family and village. Life and death would go on, the Hopis believed, as long as the sun rose and set upon the earth.

Their isolated location, in a region where few others wanted to live, helped the Hopis to keep their traditions alive for thousands of years. They lived in peace, following a clear path from birth to death. Still, the Hopi way of life was severely threatened when the Spaniards, followed by other whites, began moving into the Southwest during the 1500s.

Chapter Three

ARRIVAL OF THE "LOST WHITE BROTHER"

An ancient Hopi legend says that mankind was once united, Indian and white, and spoke the same language. One day, the Hopi elders sent their white brother, Pahana, east to the rising sun. He was told to bring back new knowledge to help his Indian brothers. Before he left, the elders gave Pahana a piece of the sacred stone tablet. When he came back, he would show it to them, so they would know he was truly their lost white brother.

A similar legend was told by the Aztecs who lived south of the Hopis, in Mexico. Strangely enough, the Spanish explorer Hernando Cortés arrived there in 1519, the same year Aztec legends had said their lost white brother, Quetzalcoatl, would come. At first the Aztecs welcomed Cortés, but the well-armed Spaniards conquered them in just fourteen years.

More Spaniards came, seeking riches in the Americas. In 1540, Francisco de Coronado and his soldiers reached the Southwest. There were then about 30,000 Pueblo Indians, of whom a few thousand were Hopis. The Zuni Pueblos were the

*When Francisco de Coronado and his men made
their way to the Southwest in the early sixteenth century,
they changed the Hopi way of life forever.*

first to meet the Spaniards, who rode into their village on horseback wearing fancy uniforms and armor. The Zunis had never
seen a white man or a horse before. They were surprised by these
strange creatures, but they welcomed them into their midst. The
Spaniards responded by stealing from them and attacking the
villagers. They brought new diseases that killed many natives.

Coronado had heard tales about cities of gold in a place called Tusayan, about 100 miles (161 kilometers) north of the Zuni. Three Hopi villages lay there. Oraibi, "the place of the rock," was the oldest one, founded in 1150 on the Antelope Mesa. A ceremonial stick was kept in the village to mark the time when Pahana was due to return. The Bear Clan of Oraibi made a line across the stick each year. It had been full for twenty years—Pahana was late.

One of Coronado's men, a Catholic priest named Pedro de Tovar, headed for Tusayan with a group of soldiers, some on horseback, and another priest, Juan de Padilla. When they reached Antelope Mesa, the Hopis came down to stare at them in amazement. Then Padilla and some of the soldiers charged at them with metal swords, and the Hopis fled back up the mesa.

The Hopis tried to make peace, bringing gifts of cotton cloth, food, and turquoise. They may also have let Tovar visit Oraibi. Hopi history says that the Bear Clan leader greeted Tovar by holding out his hand in a special way. The true Pahana would have known how to hold the Clan leader's hand in response. But Tovar did not. Instead, he thought the Hopi wanted a gift and told one of his soldiers to give him one.

The Hopis led Tovar up the mesa. Was this the long-lost white brother? Hopi history said that one day Hopi and white people would unite to combine their talents and get rid of their faults. They would share their goods and build a religion based on common truth and brotherhood. Tovar showed no interest in these things. He asked where he might find gold and other treasure. Tovar was not Pahana, the Hopis decided. They wanted the Spaniards to leave, so they described a great river that flowed nearby through an immense canyon—now called the Colorado River and the Grand Canyon. Tovar sent Don García de Cárdenas to find the river.

SPANISH RULE ▪ For forty years, the Hopis saw no more white men. But the Spanish had conquered New Mexico and were spreading throughout the Southwest. In 1583, a group led by Antonio de Espejo again came to Tusayan, looking for gold. The Hopis met the Spaniards peacefully, giving them food and gifts. Four Hopi men guided Espejo on his journey. He found no gold, but he did locate some silver deposits.

Juan de Oñate was put in charge of the region in 1598. He told the Hopis that the King of Spain now ruled the Southwest and all who lived there. The Hopis soon realized they could not win against these determined, armed white troops. They told Oñate they would not fight Spanish rule.

Yet for about thirty years no Spanish officials came to the mesas. The Hopis were not asked to pay tribute (taxes) to the Spanish king. Life continued much as before. Then the Spaniards began to send missionaries to teach the Hopis about the Catholic religion.

Starting in 1629, the Spanish worked hard to convert, or change, the Hopis' beliefs. At Oraibi and other villages, Hopis were forced to build Christian churches. In his book *Big Falling Snow*, Albert Yava wrote: "The way it was told to us, some of the big [wood] beams had to be brought from forty to fifty miles away, where there were large trees. . . . In Oraibi they can show you some long, worn grooves in the rocks that they say were made by dragging the logs. . . . The padres [priests] were quite severe with everybody and tried to get everyone to give up their old traditions and ceremonies."

The Hopis called the Spaniards *castillas*, after Castile, a Spanish city. They also called them *kachada*, "white man," or *dodagee*, "dictator." The Spaniards called the Hopis *moquis*, a name the Hopis considered an insult. In the Hopi language, *moqui* meant "dead."

Oraibi villagers hated the mission, calling it a "slave church." They were forced to provide food and fresh water for the missionaries and do other work for them. They were angry when the Spaniards mistreated Hopi women. Indians who disobeyed the Spanish were often cruelly punished.

The Franciscan order of Catholic priests founded new missions and tried to make other changes. Pueblo religious leaders were enraged as their people were pushed to change their ancient beliefs. The Hopis refused new Spanish names for their villages and resisted changing religions. When Spanish priests began to hold community baptisms, the Hopis were so angry that they killed several priests by throwing them off the cliffs.

Spanish missionaries disliked the kachina ceremonies. Hopi legends say that during the 1660s the Spaniards stopped the dances, and no rain fell. People died from famine. After Hopi spiritual leaders did the kachina dances in secret, the rain fell, convincing the Hopis their ways were right for them.

Many of the Spaniards in charge of the Southwest passed laws against the kachina dances. These rulings and ongoing efforts of the missionaries increased the Hopis' bitter feelings. By 1680, they were ready to go against their tradition of peace and fight the Spanish. They met with some men from other Pueblo groups who were planning a rebellion.

That August, men from some eastern Pueblo tribes began the historic Pueblo Revolt. The Hopis joined them, destroying several missions and killing priests, their assistants, and soldiers. They sealed the contents of the churches and the soldiers' armor and weapons in caves, says Hopi history. The villagers carried all the stones from the "slave church" out of Oraibi. They kept the wooden beams to use in their kivas. They also kept the Spaniards' cattle and sheep. From then on, the Hopis raised their own livestock and learned to weave with wool, as well as cotton.

Twenty years passed before the two peoples clashed once again. In 1700, Catholic priests began to baptize villagers at Awatovi. Soon, fights broke out between Catholic and traditional Hopis. Unable to stop the violence, the Awatovi chief and village leaders decided to destroy the entire village. They thought Awatovi was too evil and disorderly to save. That fall, bands of armed Hopi men attacked the village, burning the buildings and killing the people. Only a few women and girls were spared and sent to other villages.

The destruction of Awatovi was especially tragic because the Hopis believed people must live in harmony, with love for all living things. In order to save their own religion they had violated their deepest beliefs.

In later years, the Spanish tried to regain control of the Hopis, but they met stiff opposition. Oraibi was especially resistant. Also, because the climate was so dry, few settlers chose to live in the mesa country. Spanish ways did not gain a firm hold there, although Hopis took advantage of the material goods the

Oraibi is the oldest Hopi village. Photographed here in 1898, it is still inhabited today.

Europeans had brought. Metal tools proved useful in farming, and new crops were grown. Alfalfa, wheat, peas, beets, watermelons, chili peppers, tomatoes, lettuce, and peaches and apricots added variety to the Hopi diet. Mostly, though, the Hopis and other Pueblos kept their old ways.

Another group of settlers then came to upset the Hopis. These were the Navajos. As more Spaniards came to the region, scattered groups of Navajos were pushed onto Hopi lands from the north. They wore animal skins and had been nomads (wanderers) rather than residents of settled communities. The Navajos began to settle near the Hopi mesas in canyons that held water the Hopi had long been using. Navajo sheep and other livestock damaged Hopi fields. Hopi men began to guard their fields during harvesttime. Fights broke out between these peoples. The conflict remained heated in the early 1900s and still affects land disputes today.

THREE MESAS ▪ By the early 1800s, the Hopi people lived on the three mesas they now occupy in Arizona. On First Mesa were the villages of Walpi, Sichimovi (also Sichomove, or Sitchumovi), and Hano. People came to Walpi, "the place of the gap," in the late 1600s. They had first lived lower on the mesa, but they moved up to avoid the Spaniards.

Sichimovi, "the place of the mound where wild currants grow," was founded about 1750 by members of the Lizard, Patki, Wild Mustard, and Badger clans. Hano was not a traditional Hopi village but was founded by Tewa Pueblos. They came as refugees from the Rio Grande valley after the Pueblo Revolt. The Tewa kept their traditions, religion, and language and became known as the Hopi-Tewa.

Three villages were scattered on Second Mesa. Shongopovi, "the place by the spring where the tall reeds grow," was founded by people who had lived in the foothills below the mesa, near Gray Spring. In 1629, the Spanish built the San Bartolome mission there. When it was torn apart during the Pueblo Revolt, the people moved to the top of the mesa.

Mishongnovi, "the place of the black man," was named for Mishong, a leader of the Crow clan. It was said that he had led some people from the San Francisco Peaks region in the 1200s. They settled at Corn Rock, an ancient Hopi shrine, or sacred site. Franciscan priests built the San Buenaventura chapel there in 1629. It, too, was destroyed in 1680. The people left the village to build one in its present, higher, location.

Also on Second Mesa lay Shipolovi, "the mosquitoes," which Hopis say was settled by people from an ancient pueblo on the Little Colorado River. The people left after mosquitoes swarmed into the area. Others say Shipolovi was founded by people from Shongopovi after the Pueblo Revolt. They used it as a safe place to hold religious ceremonies.

On Third Mesa was Oraibi, the oldest of all the Hopi villages. Along with the Pueblo village of Acoma, Oraibi is thought to be the oldest continuously occupied site in the United States.

A NEW RULER ■ The 1800s brought more changes. By then, the Spanish no longer controlled the Southwest. Colonists in the East had fought the American Revolution and won their independence from Britain in 1781. By 1819, the United States Congress had passed a law that allowed money to be paid to missionaries who went to live among western tribes. From 1800 to 1825, more whites moved to the West. Besides missionaries and settlers, there were thousands of explorers, trappers, soldiers, traders, ranchers, and government agents.

With these white settlers came smallpox and other diseases unknown to Native Americans. Indians were not immune; that is, they had no natural resistance to these deadly germs. By 1853 hundreds of Hopis were stricken with smallpox. An army engineer who visited a Hopi pueblo said that "only the chief and one other man remained of all the able-bodied men in town."

By this time, the United States government had taken control of the Southwest. Some government officials cared about the Hopis and treated their culture with respect. But on the whole, government policy aimed at forcing Indians to adopt white lifestyles and the Christian religion. In 1865 a law was passed that said Indian children must be sent to boarding schools where they would learn "white ways." Four years later, a federal agent was sent to govern the Hopis. A Protestant mission school was set up in 1870 at Keam's Canyon, but most Hopis ignored it.

Until 1882 the U.S. government had not disputed the Hopis' claim to a large land area in the Southwest. In that year, the government set aside 2,428,000 acres (982,563 hectares) as the Hopi reservation. By then, many Navajos lived there, too. Hopi chiefs met with President Benjamin Harrison in Washington in 1890 to protest that this was their sacred, ancestral land. But Hopi and white ideas about ownership were very different. Often discussions led to even greater misunderstandings.

The General Allotment Act, passed in 1887, said that Indian lands were to be split into separate plots and given to individual Indians. In 1891, surveyors came to Hopi land to start dividing it. Many Hopis were so angry they tore out the surveyors' stakes. That same year, another smallpox epidemic killed more Hopis.

The U.S. government worked harder to send Indian children to government schools. Soldiers from Fort Defiance went to Or-

Native American schoolchildren at a missionary school.

aibi and removed 104 children against their will. They were sent to a boarding school. The children had to wear whites' clothing and get white-style haircuts. They were ordered to speak only English and attend Christian religious services.

As the twentieth century began, the Hopis worked hard to balance the old ways with the new. While photographing a Hopi man in the early 1900s, Indian historian Edward S. Curtis remarked, "The eyes are wary, perhaps with distrust, the mouth unyielding in stubbornness. Yet behind the mask are warm-hearted friendliness and a sense of humanity."

A Hopi brother and sister sit in front of a traditional adobe home dressed in white men's clothes.

Chapter Four

HOPIS TODAY

The arrival of whites, with their new government and different ways, threatened Hopi traditions. Yet today, some Hopis live much as their ancestors did. Others, sometimes called Progressives, have left the mesas and adopted the ways of the larger white society. Still other Hopis blend both ways of life. They may work in a city like Winslow, Arizona, but return to their ancestral villages for traditional ceremonies.

Hopi Wayne Sekaquaptewa has said, "There is no way in the world we can escape modern society, even if we build a stone wall around the reservation." Wallace Youvella, an artist from First Mesa, speaks for many Hopis when he says, "I'm a progressive, but in a way I'm still traditionalist. . . . I'm for progress—for new schools, new gas stations, for improvements in the villages—but progress has to work from the past."

By 1900, there were visible changes on the mesas. There was a new, westernmost village: Moenkopi, the "place of the running water." It had started as a farming settlement at Oraibi, then separated in the 1870s, led by Chief Tuba. It is located 40 miles (64 kilometers) west of the other Third Mesa villages and follows Oraibi traditions. Unlike other villages, Moenkopi has irrigated fields.

Kykotsmovi, "place of the hills of ruins," is also called Lower or New Oraibi. It was settled in 1890 by people from Oraibi who wanted to live closer to the trading post and school.

In 1906, Oraibi had a population of about 1,200. Its people were arguing about ceremonies and how to best deal with the U.S. Bureau of Indian Affairs. They settled the problem without bloodshed. Those who lost the argument left Oraibi with their leader, Yukioma, to start a more conservative village, Hotevilla. Yukioma and his followers asked to be left alone, but whites built a school and churches at Hotevilla anyway. Officials tried to force children to attend school. When Yukioma protested, he was sent to Keams Canyon jail.

Granado Mission was built near Keams Canyon by Presbyterians in 1901. Clarence Salsbury, a doctor, and his wife, a nurse, came there in 1926. They started a nursing school where Indians could study and then apply for a state license after their training. But many Hopis disliked the fact that Salsbury was so eager to convert them. Mennonites, Mormons, Jehovah's Witnesses, Seventh Day Adventists, and Baptists also came. Albert Yava, a Hopi-Tewa, told a missionary what he felt about this:

Maybe you have a good church. But I have been doing a lot of thinking about what you missionaries are doing, and the way you are doing it. The first thing you do is to say that the Hopi and Tewa religious practices are barbaric and after that you convince a few people here and there that they have to become Christians so as not to go to hell. But . . . you don't really know anything about what Hopis and Tewas believe in.

NEW HOPI WAYS ▪ The government was slowly changing its policy of forcing Native Americans to give up their culture, language, and religion. Even so, in 1936, it pressured all Hopi groups to unite into a single tribe. This was a foreign idea to the Hopis, who had never before had a central political authority.

By the end of that year the Hopis had approved a constitution that defined the tribe as "a union of self-governing villages, sharing common interests and working for the common welfare of all." The number of tribal representatives from each village was based on how many people lived there. Members of the Hopi Tribal Council had to be at least twenty-five years old, speak the native language, and have lived in a Hopi village for at least two years.

Some Hopis took on new jobs besides farming. Many raised cattle to increase their income. By the 1900s, about 1,200 Hopis worked outside the mesas, in Grand Canyon, Winslow, Flagstaff, and other places in Arizona. Some Hopis worked near their villages in government jobs or for the Indian Health Service and Bureau of Indian Affairs. And by 1977, the Hopi Tribal Council had given $7 million to tribal agencies that employed hundreds of people.

Many Hopi farmers have continued to follow traditional ways, even using a digging stick. In 1987, the chief administrative officer of the Hopi government, Clifford Balenquah, said, "When you plant your crops, you offer some seed to Spider Woman, some to the worms, some to the birds, and then you say, 'Whatever is left, let my family feed from that.' " Balenquah says he is progressive in some ways, but he likes to follow traditions in farming and religion.

The Hopis value education and have worked to improve their schools, located at Keams Canyon, Polacca, Second Mesa, and Hotevilla. Young people do well in their classes and some go on to junior or four-year colleges. They have made contributions in law, health care, journalism, and the arts, among other fields.

First and second graders in class at the Hotevilla Day School on a Hopi reservation in Arizona.

An example of Hopi silverwork and a stunning piece of pottery with a traditional Hopi design.

ARTS AND CRAFTS ▪ Since the late 1960s, there has been fresh interest in Native American culture and crafts. Hopi art is admired and prized by collectors. People buy kachina and other dolls, carved stone or wood ceremonial objects, pottery, silverwork, fine jewelry, weaving, and basketry. The Hopis still make plaited baskets to use and to sell. Many of these have diamond or square patterns. Wicker baskets are woven with several colors. They are often called "Oraibi baskets" but are woven on other mesas, too.

Silverwork often blends two pieces of silver. The top one has cutout patterns, while the lower one is black. They are melted together to create lovely designs.

The Hopis still do traditional weaving, using patterns from nature—clouds, lightning, sun, and rain. Other Indians come to the Hopis for the ceremonial belts they alone make.

Kachina dolls are also made in the traditional way, from roots of cottonwood trees, with a thin coating of white clay. Artists sometimes use commercial paints now, though.

In the late 1800s, Daisy Nampeyo, a famous Tewa-Hopi potter, revived the use of traditional clay and paints. Nampeyo's descendants and followers have continued her work, making beautiful pottery in traditional ways. The Hopis have succeeded in selling their work on their own, in stores, or through a tribal guild shop such as the one near Oraibi.

Music historian Natalie Curtis collected Hopi poems and songs for use in *The Indians' Book*. She noted that singing was part of daily life for men working in the fields or herding stock, for women cooking or caring for children, and for children at play. "To seize on paper the spirit of Hopi music is a task as impossible as to put on canvas the shimmer and glare of the desert," she wrote.

As highways made the mesas more accessible, visitors increased. This was both a problem and an asset. Although visitors intruded upon the privacy and quiet life-style of the Hopis, they also helped the economy. In 1971, the tribe built a Hopi Culture Center on Second Mesa. It offers attractive hotel rooms, a conference center, a restaurant, and shops filled with Hopi arts and crafts. Masked and unmasked kachina dancing was sometimes open to the public, as was a version of the Snake Dance. Hopi dancing, expressive and beautiful to watch, has always been a form of prayer, meant for the whole world as well as for the Hopis.

HOPI LANDS ▪ The Hopis do not believe that the white government and its laws have authority over them. But during the twentieth century, the Hopis have had to go to court in order to protect their land, water, and other rights. In one case, the Hopis sued a coal company that planned to strip-mine Hopi lands. Once fairly isolated on their mesas, the Hopis have recently joined other Native American tribes and the All-Indian Pueblo Council, as well as whites, to solve certain problems.

The centuries-old land dispute between the Hopis and Navajos has continued to the present. In 1937, the government took more land from the Hopis. It gave them the sole right to just 631,174 acres (255,423 hectares)—less than half of the 2.5 million acres (1 million hectares) it had given them in 1882. The rest was to be shared equally with the Navajos. Congress approved this Joint Use area. The decision was made partly because the Navajo population was growing faster than the Hopi. (By 1985, there were about 8,952 Hopis and 166,665 Navajos, with about 59 percent of them living in Arizona.)

In 1970, the Hopis asked a federal court to remove the Navajos from this "shared" area. The Indian Claims Commission awarded the Hopis payments for the estimated 5 million acres (2 million hectares) taken in 1882 and for the 1.8 million acres (.7 million hectares) that were taken in 1937. The arguments went on, so the courts tried dividing the Joint Use lands between Hopis and Navajos. Many Navajos were told to leave their homes.

The two tribes would struggle with this problem for years. In 1986, Congress said the tribes could trade certain lands if that would solve some disagreements. Then Navajos were given another year to relocate. To help them move, the U.S. government provided financial aid and housing. But, the dispute remained unsettled.

In 1988, the Association on American Indian Affairs, with both white and Indian members, began helping First Mesa villagers to restore their historic buildings and to build sanitary facilities. Walpi village got help from the National Park Service for repairs and a paved road.

The Hopis, who have always respected the earth, have shown a deep concern for the environment. A Hopi elder, Thomas Benyacya, spoke before a United Nations Conference on World Habitat and at the International Conference on the Environment in Stockholm, Sweden, in 1974. He said:

> Once all mankind was one and in harmony with its surroundings. Then our white brother separated from us and went east, across the great waters. It was said that at some time he would come back with all his great inventions to help his red brother and then we would be as one again. But our white brother misunderstood and misused his inventions which ruin the land which he no longer knows and understands. We still hope that Pahana, our white brother, will come back to us to bring peace instead of war, peace to men and peace to the earth.

The Hopis still live on the harsh, dry lands of their ancestors, raising the crops that have nourished them for thousands of years. They have managed to keep their beliefs and way of life despite the pressures of a changing world.

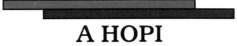

A HOPI
CREATION STORY

Long, long ago, the Underworld deep inside the earth was a huge sea. In this sea lived two goddesses, one in the East and one in the West. Their homes were much like a Hopi kiva and held many treasures—beautiful seashells and turquoise. The goddess of the East hung a yellow fox skin and a gray one at the door of her house, while the goddess of the West had a turtle-shell rattle. Early each morning, the Sun rose and put on the gray fox skin, then later, the yellow skin. After a day of moving across the Underworld, it tapped the turtle-shell rattle, then dropped into the kiva of the goddess of the West.

One day, the two goddesses decided to make some land. They pulled apart the sea so that new land appeared. Next, they decided to create living things, and made a bird from a piece of clay. This first bird, a wren, they set free to look for other life. The bird saw none, but it had overlooked Spider Woman, who lived and ruled in the Southwest.

The goddess of the West created animals, while the one in the

East made a man and a woman from clay. By singing a special song, she brought them to life. The goddess taught these new people to speak and sent them over the rainbow to the western goddess's home. When Spider Woman saw this, she asked Mockingbird to help her make some people, whom she taught different languages. These people spread throughout the Underworld. The goddess of the West made people, too, and these became the Hopis. The Hopis emerged one day from the Underworld to live on the mesas of northeastern Arizona.

The Hopis believe the entrance to the Underworld lies at the bottom of the Canyon of the Little Colorado above the spot where it joins the Colorado River.

IMPORTANT DATES

400–500   The Anasazi begin to settle in multi-family houses called *pueblos*.

1200s   The Kayenta group of Pueblo Indians move south into present-day Arizona and become Hopis.

1300–1540   The Hopis build new mesa towns and develop their special way of life.

1540   Francisco de Coronado and his soldiers reach the Southwest; Don Pedro de Tovar and soldiers arrive at the Hopi village of Oraibi on Antelope Mesa.

1583   Antonio de Espejo leads a group of Spaniards to Tusayan, looking for gold.

1598   Juan de Oñate is appointed Spanish governor of the Southwest.

1629   The Spanish increase their efforts to change the Hopis' religion; Hopis are forced to build Catholic churches.

1680   The Hopis join other Pueblo groups to fight against the Spanish in the historic Pueblo Revolt.

1700	Violence breaks out in the village of Awatovi after Catholic priests convert many Hopis to Christianity. Unable to stop the fighting, the Awatovi chief and other leaders destroy the village.
Early 1800s	Hopis settle on the three mesas they occupy today.
1850	The U.S. government gains the Southwest from Spain.
1853	Hundreds of Hopis die in a smallpox epidemic.
1865	The U.S. government establishes a policy of sending Indian children to boarding schools to learn white culture and language.
1882	The U.S. government sets aside 2,428,000 acres (982,563 hectares) as the Hopi reservation.
1887	Congress passes the General Allotment Act.
1891	Government surveyors divide Hopi land into smaller plots (allotments).
1936	The Hopis approve their tribal constitution.
1937	The U.S. government reduces the size of Hopi land to 631,174 acres (255,423 hectares), naming the rest Joint Use land for Hopis and Navajos.
1970	The Hopis sue in federal court to have the Navajos removed from Joint Use lands; the dispute and legal battles continue into the 1990s.

GLOSSARY

Anasazi. Ancestors of the Hopis and other Pueblo Indians.

chukoviki. Ceremonial loaves of bread made by steaming dough in corn-husk wrappers.

clan. The village group to which Hopis belong from birth; clan membership comes through the mother's side of the family.

kachada. The Hopi word for a white person.

kachina. A spirit being that stands for the invisible forces of life.

kikmongwi. A village chief.

kiva. An underground room, or pit house, used for religious ceremonies.

mano. A stone used for grinding corn by hand.

mesa. Flat-topped hills; means "table" in Spanish.

metate. A stone slab upon which corn is ground.

Pahana. "The lost white brother" whom Hopi legends said would one day be reunited with them.

piki. A thin wafer bread, usually made with blue cornmeal.

pit house. See *kiva.*

pueblo. Multi-family dwellings made of stone or adobe; means "people" in Spanish.

Pueblos. Native Americans, such as the Hopis or Zunis, who belong to one of the tribes that lives in pueblos.

we-la. A game in which several players toss feathered darts of different colors.

BIBLIOGRAPHY

*Books for children

Andrews, Ralph W. *Curtis' American Indians.* Seattle: Superior Publishing Company, 1962.

Applegate, Frank G. *Native Tales of New Mexico.* Philadelphia: Lippincott, 1932.

Canby, Thomas Y. "The Anasazi," *National Geographic.* November 1982, pp. 554–592.

Courlander, Harold. *Hopi Voices.* Albuquerque, N.M.: University of New Mexico Press, 1974.

Dozier, Edward P. *The Pueblo Indians of North America.* New York: Holt, Rinehart, and Winston, 1970.

Dutton, Bertha P. *American Indians of the Southwest.* Albuquerque, N.M.: University of New Mexico Press, 1983.

*Erdoes, Richard. *The Rain Dance People.* New York: Knopf, 1976.

*Hirschfelder, Arlene. *Happily May I Walk.* New York: Scribner's, 1986.

James, Harry C. *Pages From Hopi History.* Tucson, Arizona: The University of Arizona Press, 1974.

Johnson, Trebbe. "Between Sacred Mountains: The Hopi and Navajo Concept of Peace," *Amicus Journal,* Summer 1987, pp. 18–23.

Josephy, Alvin M. *The Indian Heritage of North America.* New York: Knopf, 1968.

Kammer, Jerry. *The Second Long Walk: The Navajo Hopi Land Dispute.* Albuquerque, N.M.: University of New Mexico Press, 1980.

*Liptak, Karen. *Indians of the Southwest.* New York: Facts On File, 1991.

Page, Jake. "Inside the Sacred Hopi Homeland." *National Geographic,* November 1982, pp. 607–629.

Talayeswa, Don. *Sun Chief: The Autobiography of a Hopi Indian.* New Haven, Conn.: Yale University Press, 1942.

*Tanner, Clara Lee. *Southwest Indian Craft Arts.* Tucson, Arizona: University of Arizona Press, 1975.

Underhill, Ruth. *Workaday Life of the Pueblos.* Washington, D.C.: United States Indian Service, 1946.

Waters, Frank. *Book of the Hopi.* New York: Viking Penguin, 1963.

Weaver, Thomas. *Indians of Arizona.* Phoenix, Arizona: University of Arizona Press, 1974.

Yava, Albert (ed: Harold Courlander). *Big Falling Snow: A Tewa-Hopi Indian's Life and Times and the History and Traditions of His People.* New York: Crown, 1978.

INDEX

Page numbers in *italics* refer to illustrations.

Acoma village, 43
All-Indian Pueblo Council, 53
Anasazi Indians, 9–10, *11*, 26
Animals, 8–9, 20
Association on American Indian Affairs, 54
Awatovi village, 40
Aztec Indians, 19, 35
Aztec Tanoan language, 12

Balenquah, Clifford, 49–50
Basket Makers, 9
Basketry, 33, 51
Benyacya, Thomas, 54
Betatakin Ruin, 12
Big Falling Snow (Yava), 38
Boarding schools, 44, *45*
Bread, 20
Bureau of Indian Affairs, 48, 49

Cárdenas, García de, 38
Catholic religion, 38–40
Children, 24–28, *25*
Clan membership, 14
Climate, 9
Clothing, 20–21
Corn Rock, 43
Coronado, Francisco de, 35, *36*, 37
Cortés, Hernando, 35
Courting, 21, 23
Cradleboards, 26
Crafts, 32–34, *51*, 51–52
Creation story, 55–56
Crops, 10, 19, 41
Curtis, Edward S., 45
Curtis, Natalie, 52

Dances, 28, *29*, 30–31, *31*, 39, 52
Death, 34
Desert Culture, 9
Diseases, 36, 44

Doll-making, 32–33, 52

Education, 44–45, *45*, 50, *50*
Elderly, 10, 34
Espejo, Antonio de, 38

Family life, 15–16
Farming, 7, 12, 19, 41, 49
Food, 9, 10, 16, 18–20
Franciscans, 39
Furnishings, 14

General Allotment Act of 1887, 44
Government policies, 44–45, 47–
    49, 53–54
Granado Mission, 48
Grand Canyon, 8, 12, 38, 56

Hano village, 42
Harrison, Benjamin, 44
Hopi Indians
    children, 24–28, *25*
    clothing, 20–21
    crafts, 32–34, *51*, 51–52
    diseases, 44
    education, 44–45, *45*, 50, *50*
    elderly, 10, 34
    family life, 15–16
    farming, 7, 12, 19, 41, 49
    food, 16, 18–20
    geographic regions, 8, 9
    government policies, 44–45,
        47–49, 53–54
    houses, 14–15, *15*
    marriage, 15–16, 21, *22*, 23–
        24
    Navajos and, 42, 53

Hopi Indians (*continued*)
    Progressives, 47
    religious beliefs, 7–8, 12, 13,
        26–32, 38–40, 48–49, 55–
        56
    Spaniards and, 37–40
    villages, 12–14, 42–43, 47–
        48
    women, 15–16, *17*, 19–21
Hopi-Tewa Indians, 42
Hopi Tribal Council, 49
Hotevilla village, 48
Houses, 10, *11*, 14–15, *15*
Hunting, 20, 21, *21*

Indian Claims Commission, 53
Indian Health Service, 49

Kachinas, 28, *29*, *32*, 39, 52
Kayenta group, 10
Kivas, 13, 27
Kykotsmovi village, 48

Language, 12
Leigh, William R., *17*

Marriage, 15–16, 21, *22*, 23–24
Massau, 12
Mesa villages, *6*, 8, 12–14, 42–43,
    47–48
Mishong, 43
Mishongnovi village, 43
Missionaries, 38–40, 43, 48
Moenkopi village, 47–48

Naming ceremony, 25
Nampeyo, Daisy, 52

Navajo Indians, 42, 44, 53

Oñate, Juan de, 38
Oraibi village, 37–40, *41*, 43–45, 47

Padilla, Juan de, 37
Pahana, 35, 37, 54
Painted Desert, 8
Pottery, 33–34, *51*, 52
Progressives, 47
Pueblo Indians, 8, 9, 10, 20, 35
Pueblo Revolt, 40, 42, 43
Pueblos (houses), 10, *11*, 14–15, *15*

Quetzalcoatl, 35

Rabbit hunts, 20, 21
Rainfall, 7, 30, 31, 39
Recipes, 18
Religious beliefs, 7–8, 10, 12, 13, 26–32, 38–40, 48–49, 55–56

Salsbury, Clarence, 48
Sekaquaptewa, Wayne, 47
Shipolovi village, 43

Shongopovi village, 42–43
Sichimovi village, 42
Silverwork, 51, *51*
Smallpox, 44
Snake Dance, 30–31, *31*, 52
Spaniards, 34–40
Star People, 12
Sun Chief (Talayeswa), 7, 27

Talayeswa, Don, 7, 27
Tewa Indians, 42, 48, 49
Tools, 14–15, 41
Tovar, Pedro de, 37
Tuba, Chief, 48
Tusayan, 37, 38

Villages, *6*, 8, 12–14, 42–43, 47–48

Walpi village, *6*, 42, 54
Women, 15–16, *17*, 19–21

Yava, Albert, 38, 48–49
Youvella, Wallace, 47
Yukioma, 48

Zuni Indians, 35–36